THE GREATEST MYTH OF ADULT CHILDREN OF ALCOHOLICS, VIOLENCE, & DYSFUNCTION

We Were Loved

Michael Williams

Published by

Dysfunctional Child Publishing

williamsmike4171930@gmail.com
Escondido, California

First Printing, 2017

Printed in the United States of America

ISBN:10: 06928220485
ISBN-13: 978-0692820483

THANK YOU FOR YOUR INVESTMENT IN THIS BOOK. YOU CAN LOCATE OTHER BOOKS BY THIS AUTHOR AT WWW.AMAZON.COM OR FOLLOW THIS AUTHOR FOR NEW EDITIONS, NEW BOOKS, SPEAKIMG ENGAGEMENTS, AND SPECIAL EVENTS.

DEDICATION

My daddy was courageous on the day he told me he never loved me—his integrity and his truth changed my life forever. *He assisted me into reality* when he said, "All I ever cared about was where was my next drink coming from." In that split moment everything at long last finally made sense. It felt better than good; it felt honest; it felt sane!

This book is devoted to my drunken daddy who never loved me, and to adult children of alcoholics, violence, and dysfunction who survived a childhood without parental love.

PREFACE

The parental love we received in childhood is the root of the role, quality, and quantity of love we create throughout our entire lives. Love is a language. We can communicate only with people who speak the same language. When alcoholism, violence, and dysfunction are the educational foundations for our loving relationships, we can expect proportional consequences.

Our ability to see and interpret reality in adulthood is relative to the instructive models of our formative years. Without intervention, most of us live out the legacy of scripts we received as children. How could we reasonably be expected do anything else? It is our grooming, family tradition, and inheritance.

This book shifts the plot from one of injured child to one of enduring love.

ACKNOWLEDGEMENTS

In grateful acknowledgement to Patsy Fletcher, Denise Rhodes, Wendy Dan, L.C.S.W., and Maya Klein, Ph.D., for believing in and supporting the work.

Special thanks to Kimberly Simmons, Kirk Simmons & Kunwardip Mooker for IT support.

OTHER BOOKS BY MICHAEL WILLIAMS

GROWING UP IN ALCOHOLISM, VIOLENCE & DYSFUNCTION

LISTENING TO MY INNER CHILD

PAPERBACK AND KINDLE

THE WORKBOOK FOR GROWING UP IN ALCOHOLISM, VIOLENCE & DYSFUNCTION

WAKENING & LISTENING TO MY INNER CHILD

PAPERBACK

INSPIRATIONAL STORIES OF THE HOMELESS

DIGNITY, NOBILITY, DECENCY

PAPERBACK AND KINDLE

CURRENTLY AVAILABLE AT
WWW.AMAZON.COM

CONTENTS

Chapter One

My Daddy Told Me He Never Loved Me

My greatest myth during my childhood was the idea I was loved. The child I once was had a fervent need to be loved. I see why only now.

That fantasy enabled me to survive the chaos of the alcoholism, the violence, and the dysfunction.

I held onto the idea through the most violent beatings, the most obvious signs of neglect e.g., a parent forgetting my tenth birthday or, the most repugnant of experiences, tasting my daddy's blood splashing into my mouth during a knifing by my mother. That I was loved is a conviction I held onto beyond all reasonable cost.

During childhood my daddy rarely told me he loved me. I am at a loss to remember one incident. My mama said it all the time. Her most ardent declarations were typically subsequent to a beating she had delivered, as I was trying to stop the bleeding. Being beaten to bleeding meant I was loved throughout my childhood.

This is the historical perspective from which I listened to my father communicate to me his truth concerning his not loving his family, as described in my first book:

> In a way, I had again become that
> child hoping that he would rescue
> me and make sense out of a life

that seemed to have no sense, meaning, or purpose. He spoke gently and quietly as he said, Michael, when you were a child I never cared about you, your mother, your sister, or your brother. All I ever cared about was where was my next drink coming from.

I asked, "Did you ever love me?" He looked at me fleetingly, never quite catching my eye, and said, "No, I never loved you." Then he looked at me and said, "You know I really fucked up and I feel like I fucked you up and I want you to know that I'm sorry.

I don't know if it was what my father said that day or the way that he said it. He had this air of sadness, loss, and desperation when he said, No, I really fucked up and I want you to know that I'm sorry." I don't know if I have ever loved my father as much during my life as I did in that moment.

Here was this man whose love I wanted more than life itself telling me that he never loved me and

> that he did not care about me and somehow I was falling in love with him all over again.
>
> I stood up, grabbed his hand, and pulled him close to me and we just stood there for a moment holding onto each other. I held him while patting his back and said, "I love you," as he said, "Yeah me too." Which was his way of saying he loved me. I wanted him to say I love you and I miss you, but somehow I knew his "yeah, me too" was his way, and for the first time in my life I was realizing that in that moment he was loving me as much as he was capable of loving me.

The paragraphs above are from my first book, "Growing Up In Alcoholism, Violence, & Dysfunction," or first edition, "Earning My Parents' Love." I have been questioned concerning this passage more than any other.

There are a myriad of responses to my father's expression of his truth. The most frequent is surely he was wrong, he had to love you, he was your father. The second most common response is, "Poor Michael, you were not loved." Then there is the intellectualization, the rationalization, or minimization of his truth. None of these responses have ever been helpful to me!

Each response in its own way seeks to minimize or avoid an unkind reality, as opposed to assisting me to own, talk, and walk through the reality. As a result, I do not get to deal with the core truth of the reality and its nuances with a beloved witness, which makes it impossible to heal, since the situation is never dealt with in totality. It becomes a covert form of denial under the guise of support, when in truth it is a covert form of avoidance, because the subject is too uncomfortable to own or talk through.

The assumption that surely he was wrong has unusual implications: he lied intentionally, which would assume deliberate cruelty. Unintentional cruelty could also be a possibility however both are implications of emotional or psychological illness. I am at a loss as to why intentional or unintentional cruelty are subjective realities that are easier for many than the reality that he was sharing his truth with his son for the first time in his life as best he knew how.

If I am to trust my instincts, the latter is certainly what it felt like in the moment. I have always suspected that in that moment I felt good because for the first time in our lives as father and son we were actually sharing an intimate truth. The paradox of that experience is that in that moment I felt closer to him than I ever had.

The other most often response of "Poor Michael" bestows pity at a time when it is not needed or desired. I have already lived through the situation; I do not need pity for what went before. Recognizing the difficulty of the struggle would be more useful. It is a point of awareness or recognition rarely openly discussed.

This leads to overwhelming feelings of loneliness, since in

either situation I am left alone to deal with a brutal reality, since those who care for me the most are frequently incapable of standing in the midst of the reality with me.

Healing is rarely an alone event. It often needs to be shared and witnessed by another; however, often in an effort to save me the severity of the reality those who love me the most attempt to spare my feelings. What I need is someone to be with me as I talk through the feelings of a callous reality. In effect, I get abandoned at the very time I need support, while dealing with the challenges of walking through a brutal truth by talking.

I have learned a saying that I like a lot in my healing journey: "Sometimes reality is shitty, but it's all we got."
The reality that appears to be considered least is that sometimes parents are incapable of love. Just because one is biologically capable of procreating does not mean that individual has the emotional, mental, and spiritual wherewithal to bestow the constant and continual love that is necessary for effective parenting.

I know that is what my father was saying to me that day. In that moment he was telling me his truth. It was not only his perception; it was my own and had been suspected throughout childhood. That is the reason it felt like such a relief to hear the words that he never loved me. While I was being raised, the child I once was never felt loved.

The conflict between feeling and what was said caused incessant insanity in childhood.

I never felt loved because loving actions were rarely a reality at that point in my childhood, I often felt and believed that love was a feeling. I have since grown to know and believe that true love is not only a feeling. It is an action. True love is not a noun, it is a verb.

This is the teaching of every spiritual program I have ever been exposed to: however the child I once was believed that love was a feeling, which allowed those I depended on the most to ignore the needs of their children and continue to describe that behavior as love. Allowing one's children to go hungry was love. Beating one's children or husband was described as love. Cursing one out was described as love. Neglect was described as love. Child abuse and molestation were described as love.

As I state in my first book, we were so concerned with the way we wanted things to be, needed things to be, thought things should be, we rarely considered the way things actually were. Our reality was a stated declaration that had nothing to do with behaviors. It was as if we thought we could shape reality with words, declarations, thoughts, and feelings. The words, thoughts, and feelings were always devoid of dependable, substantial behaviors or deeds that supported the purported love.

As a child I may have had little, if any, sense of understanding and little knowledge; however what I always had was a keen sense of emotions. In many respects I suspect as a child my sense of emotional radar was even greater than as an adult, since I had not yet developed emotional defenses. So in many respects childhood was a time of pure or at least purer emotions.

This sense of emotionality is clearly illustrated from a quote from my first book, "Earning My Parents' Love" or the second edition "Growing Up In Alcoholism, Violence, & Dysfunction":

> It seems that from my earliest memories of my father they have always been involved with the feelings of longing, wanting, and desiring. My daddy's favorite place when I was a child was a place named the Five "0" Lounge, or as he affectionately referred to it, the 'Fifty Bar." I can remember many courageous trips I took in search of my daddy to the Five "0" Lounge. Each time I would seem to be filled with fear that overwhelmed me and sought to destroy my mission. In retrospect I think that my expeditions would have been easier if I had been old enough or tall enough to see over the bar. I can remember many days opening that huge door that seemed to weigh as much as I did
> and walking inside the smoke-filled room scared to death. I'm not sure what I was afraid of; all I know is I was scared. I remember walking from chair to chair asking, "You seen Pete Williams?

Have you seen Pete Williams?

The adults were big and tall and they sat on these tall stools that I had difficulty climbing up onto. I guess, in retrospect, I should be grateful. As I got older I grew to look more like my daddy. People would look at me and automatically say, "You're Pete's boy, aren't you?" This made my searching easier.

It was in front of the Fifty Bar that I learned an important lesson in life. I learned that I had the ability to do wrong. Before this incident I don't believe that it ever had occurred to me that I could do something wrong.

Being held in my daddy's arms had always been a respite for me. It was a place of sheer joy at just being me. It was in front of the Fifty Bar that I realized I had committed my first sin – although inadvertent it may have been, it was a sin nonetheless.
I stared up into my daddy's big brown eyes admiring his huge shoulders and arms and I said,

"Daddy, pick me up." A bit louder the second time: "Daddy, pick me up." Finally, while tugging on his fingers: "Daddy, pick me up?" He looked into my eyes and said, "Michael, no, you're getting too big to pick up," and I realized I had committed my first sin – I had grown. Until this day, I still remember that feeling of a knife twisting and stabbing at my heart. I was utterly defenseless to protect myself from its sheer stabbing and jabbing as it laid me open to the cruel New Jersey wind on that gusty autumn day.

Although I did not know it at the time, I think I felt my first feelings of jealousy that day. I was jealous of whatever he did at the Fifty Bar that put that glazed look in his eyes, which he loved more than he loved me.

I don't remember ever asking my daddy to pick me up again. I would hold onto his fingers sometimes, or play in his hair, or gaze at him longingly, or when I became older rub my shoulder next to his, but I never again asked him to pick me up.

There is something I lost that day in front of the Five "0" Lounge that I have struggled to regain my entire life. That something was not small, just I was no longer small. I lost my sense of innocence. That lost sense of innocence would accompany me throughout the next few years as my search for my daddy would take me through floating crap games, poker games, and more bars as the years progressed. In each place, I would always be greeted with the same salutation: "Hey, you're Pete's boy, aren't you?"

Searching for my daddy became a skill which the family would depend upon more as the years went by. I learned many things while searching for my daddy. I learned how to ride the bus system in New Jersey. I learned how to navigate the New York City subway system. I learned how to locate and enter a floating crap game without getting cut by the lookout. I learned how to get information from the drunks without their

> robbing me, and I learned how to develop a way out of every situation at the same time I was also developing a way in.

Although I was obviously still a small child it was obvious I was jealous. I was jealous of my father's first love. I was jealous of whatever put that glazed look in his eyes at the Fifty Bar. I was jealous of his drinking.

That small story from my first book describes me in search of my father not only physically but on a deeper level. I was a child who was in search of my father's love, attention, adoration, and time. On the day my daddy told me that he never loved me he explained to me why all those efforts had failed. I had always been in search of something that never existed, because my daddy had never loved me. I was a child ceaselessly and often perilously searching for a father's emotional availability that was never there.

Chapter Two

My Mama Said She Always Loved Me

My experiences of "love" concerning my mother were quite different than my experiences with my father. Below is a quote from my first book:

> By the time, I entered high school I was convinced my mother hated me. I wasn't sure why, but in my heart of hearts I believed that she did. In my mind, it was not so much anything I had done, it was more of sense of who I was as a person. I questioned and often regretted that I existed. I was convinced that my existence caused my mother pain. There was no single act that persuaded me, but more a series of acts over a long period of time that had overwhelmed me, moving me to that point.
>
> There was this place in my heart that I felt only she could fulfill. I spent most of my childhood and adult life trying to fill that place and I never did. In my heart, there was a longing for her and

eventually a mourning of her.

This realization that I made no later than age thirteen was intense and sad for the child that I was. My life's experiences had convinced me that my mother hated me. I was not who she wanted me to be, needed me to be, or who I should have been according to her. This led to a profound self-loathing. I projected onto myself the hatred I felt from her. The sense that my existence caused my mother pain was a dilemma from which there was no way out.

I could withstand the violence, the beatings, and the arguments that I witnessed and was a part of as a child. Horrible as they may have been, I had developed ways to survive, withstand, and tolerate that terrible sense of ambiguity that I lived with as a child. What I could not withstand and what I believe to this day threatened the survival of my soul was that terrible sense of dispossession. That sense that my life, my soul, my essence, and my survival

> belonged, not to me, but to someone else. There was a sense of futile hostility that I was unable to stop. That sense that, as my mama stared into my eyes and raced back past everything I had ever learned to do to protect myself, at some point I would cease to exist. To this, I was totally defenseless and feared more than any other act.

I believed the person I loved the most next to my father was dangerous, hostile, and resentful of my existence. This made my existence in that house a child's nightmare. I was not a child who you could take by the hand and gently lead to look under the bed to prove there were no monsters in the house, because there were monsters in the house I grew up in.

I comment in my first book:

> My mother once said something to me I remember. She said, 'I did the best that I could.' I don't know why I remember that statement but I do. That statement brings up more questions than answers for me though. How did I come to witness so many acts of violence? Why was it that the police came to our house so many times, and,

> especially, how did I get cut by my own mama while she was fighting my father? The most important questions, though, are why did I never feel loved? Why was I always so scared? Why was I so confused and so alone?

It took quite a bit of time to discover what appeared to be my inadvertent intense anger concerning that statement until one day it came to me.

That statement was made soon after the day my father had admitted his truth to me that he never loved me. His truth was a relief, and it brought sanity into my life and it helped me into reality. His courage that day was one of the greatest gifts of my life. It improved the quality of my life forever. It set me free to search for new definitions of love, less painful definitions.

He affirmed all of the questioning feelings I had concerning my childhood with one statement. He made everything finally make sense, and since things made sense it was a relief from the incessant conflicting realities I had been raised with because love was no longer entwined with unrelenting pain.

The people I loved the most, depended upon the most, trusted the most, and loved the most were the ones who repeatedly caused the most pain. It was a horrendous childhood. There was nowhere to run, because the people who would have been the ones to run to for protection were the people who were causing the pain. That was the fundamental nature of my dilemma of insanity.

When my father told me he had never loved me or our family, that was a radical departure from the historical perspective of my childhood desires to believe.

It felt new and different because it *was* new and different, and for that I am and will always be grateful. The new reality that he led me into that day was a step in growth for both him and me and the seed planted that day has never ceased to grow into an ever widening and expansive new definition of love.

When my mother told me she did the best that she could, I came to understand my anger. I asked her the same question that I had asked my father: "Did you ever love me?" Her answer that "she did the best that she could" *did not answer the question I presented.*

My question was to ascertain information that would help me to understand and accept the pain of childhood. Her answer that she did the best that she could changes the direction from a question designed to nurture and support the child that I once was and the adult I had become to a question that is altered to provide comfort and pity for the effort she had made during my childhood. *It takes the attention off of me and puts it on her,* while I am attempting to concentrate on myself. It leads me in a direction of co-dependence.

This redirection then becomes a subtle inadvertent repeat of my childhood, because I am no longer centering on my own needs and emotions, but now concentrating on her needs and emotions. Even as an adult I had been manipulated to taking care of my parent as opposed to continue the questioning of my parent toward my own, care, nurture, and support.

While it may have been inadvertent, it was also covert and manipulative and that is the essence of my anger, because it is a continuation of the insanity that I grew up with. The children who are least equipped to care, nurture, and support are constantly manipulated into caring, nurturing, and supporting our parents.

This was, in a way, the beginning of the end of what little relationship I had with my mother, because I came to realize there was no way to continue to be in relationship with her other than to continue her narrow interpretation of reality as she saw it, which was now growing in opposition to my own.

Her interpretation presented a continuation of a childhood insanity that I not only had grown weary of, but had now begun to seek ways out of. So while it was the beginning of the end concerning her, my father provided me with a new way of looking at things, which developed into a new bloom in the flower of my life that was now growing.

Chapter Three

Childhood Is Where I Learned How To Love

I grew up without a realistic, convincing, or trustworthy experience of love, which left me ignorant to the ability, capacity, and nature of love, and its many nuances. This deficit supported a craving for love throughout adulthood; the craving overwhelmed many life behaviors including common sense. This absence of childhood loving directly contributed to a lack of balance as an adult.

Many of the behaviors defined as love in childhood involved unrelenting pain. This had been my model of love from which my childhood educational experiences of love stem. Consequently, I was often unable to determine a potentially loving situation from a painful circumstance, since for me they were and had always been inextricably entwined. This fashioned an inability to analyze and evaluate myself in basic situations of human interactions.

I endured painful situations that were not healthy because I could not readily identify the difference between a painful situation and a loving circumstance that needed to be worked on and talked through, that held some functional or useful potential. The endurance of pain had been the story of my childhood, so there was no reason why I should have questioned the continuation of this occurrence in adulthood.

Since the parental or caregiver relationship is the critical model of behavior, those of us raised by alcoholic, violent, or dysfunctional caregivers generally lack realistic and trustworthy experiences of love. We lack the experience of loving, meaningful, and significant relationships. As a result we can often initiate fantasy as a replacement, since it is always within our grasp. We cannot emulate that which we have not experienced.

Those of us raised in alcoholic, violent, or dysfunctional homes often are trying to maneuver our way through life unaware that we are, in effect, emotionally disabled. Similar to other forms of disability, we are often immobilized or rendered inoperative because we lack the mental, emotional, or spiritual tools from which to move forward.

Like any other skill in life that has been unobserved, untaught, or rarely practiced, we are not going to be competent or functional at recognizing, nurturing, and sustaining loving relationships in a proficient manner, since we lack the cumulative experiences, models, and education that nurture and support a mature attitude concerning relationships.

The alcoholic, violent, or dysfunctional family centers on the dysfunctions as opposed to the children. As a result, most adults raised in this situation have little experience with identifying, navigating, and communicating our own emotions.

In childhood my experience was that my daily emotional concentrations and worries were always centered on my drunken father or my mentally ill mother. Misinterpreting or missing the emotional state of my parents would often result in dire consequences; as a result I was often left with negligible energy for the consideration of my own emotions. It developed an ability to emotionally live outside of myself with a predisposition to other people's emotions and little regard for my own.

I was oblivious to this lack of self-familiarity to the degree that it became a core issue. Self-unfamiliarity was a consequence of years of unconscious co-dependent behavior that was not only necessary, but critical to maintain the status quo of an alcoholic household that was riddled with violence and beleaguered with dysfunction.

Lack of experience and guidance of effective parenting created a skill deficiency in navigating life's circumstances that was compounded by my unfamiliarity with being able to talk through my own challenging emotions. I had neither the experience of a growing maturity and few experiences without the influence of alcohol, denial, or delusion. In my case this circumstance provided wonderfully fertile ground for the fantasies of love to take root. These fantasies were rarely based upon wisdom, discipline, spirituality, or experience and strongly based upon the way I needed it to be, wanted it to be, or thought it should be, as had been my family experience or foundation.

My life was becoming an emotional repeat of childhood; however, how could it not? It was all I knew. That which was unknown concerning my childhood guaranteed a repeat of my childhood. This fact may well illustrate the need for truth more than any other.

The essence of most dysfunctions, whether it is alcohol, drug addiction, violence, or any other dysfunction is denial of the dysfunction. As a result, those of us who grew up in dysfunction have had an in-depth education in ignoring not only reality but especially emotions and most particularly our own emotions, because we were children and had no power. The denial of emotional truth is the perfect cultivation of the spiritual, emotional, and mental soil of a fantasy world typically described as emotional defenses; some may even label it as delusional.

For those of us who grew up with violence, our schooling was to ignore reality or face the violent consequences from parents who were not above beating their children for the presentation or confrontation of uncomfortable truths or realities.

Since we are unaware of the fact that we are emotionally disabled we tend to deny ourselves the most basic of considerations, kindness, and tenderness.

We don't recognize love, the kind of love, when and how to act upon love, or to be paralyzed the very moment when action is needed or to act at the very moment when we need to be still and allow reality to unfold.

Rarely experiencing true love during childhood left me at a considerable loss in recognizing the seeds of love later in life. What it felt like. What it looked like. Or, most importantly, what was its function. Since love in my childhood rarely served a function, it became normal in adulthood also for it rarely to serve a function, so the comfort, nurture, and support of loving relationships was often lacking in those very relationships that I would define as loving. In fact, quite to the contrary, these often would be the relationships that would provide the most emotional strife just as those relationships in my family of origin. It is all I knew.

The idea of a loving relationship being a respite, a peaceful home of support, nurture, and fuel, devoid of harmful critique, demeaning innuendo or constant judgment was an experience beyond my own, so therefore it was challenging even to image what had not been modeled and or more importantly experienced. How does one imagine or emulate that which has not been experienced or discovered?

My childhood taught me to choose relationships that were verbally declared as love, as if the declaration was the making of the reality; however, there were not many behaviors that could easily be recognized as loving. Since childhood was often and more than likely lacking loving behaviors this felt normal based upon my historical past.

Attempting to live a functional adult life without benefit of the capacity of love puts one at a staggering disadvantage in attempting to live at least a minimally functional life. Life can easily become a series of adolescent idealisms based upon fantasy as opposed to any behavior-modeled realities.

Childhood in an alcoholic or violent home lacks, above all a sense of balance. Family and love are rarely paramount issues. Alcohol, violence, or dysfunction supersedes all else. Therefore children remain without a sense of balance or a dependable or functional model of familial balance on which to rely. As a result, what the adult child from an alcoholic home often perceives as balance is rarely effective.

In the alcoholic home the children often act as adults, leaving the adult child without a realistic sense of control, power, or influence. This lends itself to enduring dysfunctional relationships far longer than necessary or reasonable. However as adult children of an alcoholic we do not see it because we were trained not to see. If we did engage the caregivers of our childhoods, we received unrelenting instructions, advice, and support on how not to believe the reality of our own perceptions.

This learned skill of being unable to see, identify, or recognize functional love tends to become a trait of life. As a result, as we grow older we often try harder in situations that are useless. In short, the older we become and the harder we try, the more blind we become, often leading to disillusionment, desperation and simply giving up on the hope, need, and humanity of human closeness. This is a horrendous price to pay for parental alcoholism, violence, and dysfunction.

The emotional skill of being unable to see what is directly in front of one's face is a finely tuned practice for those of us who grew up with alcoholism, violence, and dysfunction.

Parental alcoholics or caregivers have less ability to deal with reality than the children they are raising, so the children learn how to shield the parents from the reality they see sometimes daily. If or when the child confronts an alcoholic parent over drinking that they perceive may be detrimental to the family, the consequences for the child could be anything from denial, to verbal abuse, to physical abuse. As a result, the child's inability to see what is directly in front of him or her or to deny it becomes a paramount survival skill. It serves a vital function as long as the child is in that environment. This creates a special kind of neurosis in the adult child of an alcoholic, who had years of being trained not to see.

The ability of the adults not to see often places adult responsibilities on the shoulders of the children. Adult responsibility while still in the body of a child creates neurosis.

When the adult-child leaves such an environment, the ingrained survival skills do not stop. It is ingrained and has served the individual well for years, therefore it tends to continue as a way of life. This becomes one of the most crippling behaviors, once again rendering most adult children of alcoholics emotionally disabled.

We were not trained to utilize the information that emotions give us about ourselves in order to make informed decisions. We were trained to ignore the very information we need in order to make highly intuitive and useful decisions.

It is in this dysfunctional environment that children learn to deny the truth. Moreover, they learn to deny the most pertinent truth to the effective functioning of the family and to the child. Therefore, as an adult, that training tends to assist us in denying the most pertinent information we need to access in order to make knowledgeable decisions concerning ourselves throughout our adult life.

If the consequences for the child are verbal or physical abuse, then this denial becomes a necessary skill for survival that is highly ingrained and often exists on an unconscious level to the child, because it is all the child has ever known. This is the insidious nature of the denial of reality for adult children of alcoholics.

This skill tends to exist unconsciously. We are left

attempting to live life partially blinded to reality. *The consequences of our blinded illusions are always more painful than the reality.*

Chapter Four

Parental Love Created Separation

The profound sense of isolation and separation of growing up in an alcoholic, violent, or dysfunctional home is not easy to describe.

During childhood there was this part of my father that I was unable to reach. It felt as if I longed for something from him that I sometimes was able to approach, however never really arrived at. It revealed itself in my need to be noticed, my need for someone to talk to who was at least interested in me, or simply my need for attention from a concerned loved one. My childhood was without these elements of humanity.

It left a hole in my heart and it felt as if it was growing when I was in stressful situations. My father could never assist me in molding and developing myself because he had never molded or developed himself. So he passed to me what he had, which was inadequate not only for me but for him since he never knew how to live outside of a constant state of drunkenness.

If the purpose of childhood is to play, explore, develop, and mature and to learn for self-developmental reasons for later challenges in life, those of us who grew in alcoholism, violence, and dysfunction were on our own. We had no guide.

Consequently, I was left to deal with the challenges of growing up by myself and to figure things out as best I could with no one to rely on. Worse yet, when my father did attempt to assist, often his guidance was without any demonstrated behavior to lend credibility which raised doubt in my adolescent mind.

There were times when I would follow his guidance and discover he knew nothing of what he was talking about, and he often made a bad situation worse. That occurred so often that by the time I was a teenager I neither respected nor wanted his opinion on most things. My lack of regard stemmed from two things: a lack of respect for what he was doing with his own life, and more importantly, it was extremely challenging to my adolescent mind to respect this individual who I would so often see drunk. I saw him as powerless, and weak. As a result I often felt he needed my help more than I needed his.

I once heard someone say that as he got older his father got smarter. That has never been my truth. As I got older my father got drunker. I started to realize more and more all the ways in which I needed competent adult guidance and leadership and rarely received it.

This idea of figuring things out on my own was a bad precedent for a successful life in those times where life is a collaboration. Being in relationship is a sign of collaboration at some level and many things are based upon relationships, family, friends, jobs, religions, recreational activities, and more. As a result of growing up emotionally isolated, the idea of being in relationship was not only an intellectual challenge, it was a life skill I had no model to draw upon and, worse yet, a deficiency of experiences from which wisdom is acquired.

Since life is collaborative, there can be enduring consequences of growing up with the profound sense of isolation because of alcoholic parents. They are:

1. Weakened relationship experiences
2. No functional relationship models
3. A lack of collaborative experiences and models
4. An inability to recognize when assistance is needed
5. An inability to effectively ask for help, especially from those we view as authority figures
6. An inability to be comfortable with vulnerability

These are simply some of the consequences of growing up with a sense of being alone.

Alcoholism has robbed us of emotional connection from those we depended upon the most to demonstrate the how, why, when, and where of human connectedness.

What remains is an exaggerated sense of self-reliance, as opposed to a realistic and balanced sense of self. We are left with few, if any childhood experiences of connectedness during periods of stress or challenge, so the idea of human connectedness as a method of human soothing and comfort tends to be beyond our ability to perceive, let alone achieve. More than half my life was over prior to my making these realizations, which is another sadness in and of itself.

A lack of awareness of the potential of human connectedness has enduring consequences throughout a lifetime. The lack of a model and questions not unanswered but unasked became a recipe for an enduring life of emotional aloneness. The loneliness of alcoholism is inadvertently passed from one generation to the next and endures for the life of the generation unless treated.

Even when active drinking may disappear from the family lineage, the emotional consequences tend to linger for generations making treatment or diagnosis that much more complicated. This is one of many unintended consequences of alcoholism.

Chapter Five

Childhood's Legacy of Love

An undeniable inheritance of growing up in an alcoholic, dysfunctional, or violent home is an ingrained challenge of being able to recognize, develop, sustain, give, and accept love. Having parents who are relatively helpless predisposes children to be able to give what they identify as love due to parental neediness and demands. However it incapacitates those children for the experience of receiving love because it tends to be a practice beyond our awareness and experiences. *Infrequency of the reception of loving experiences rarely nurtures an intuitive instincts for the reception of love.*

It is similar to becoming an adult and attempting to speak a foreign language without ever having heard the language. Complicating the situation is the fact that the skills discussed here are usually required prior to an adult child even knowing there is a deficit in the proficiency level.

My knowledge of love had more to do with what I thought it should be, wanted it to be, needed it to be, what I had overheard, saw on media and hardly ever came from an acute entrenched experience of love and/or meaningful and significant experiential relationship interactions with parents. Without the root of love within ones soul it becomes an unreasonable expectation for the flowering of a loving experience without ever having had a seed planted.

Since adult children of alcoholics tend to judge ourselves without mercy, we then proceed to another ingrained lesson from childhood, which is to participate in judgment for perceived failure either by judging ourselves or our partners. Hardly ever does it occur to us that maybe, just maybe, we are seeking to accomplish a task for which we were, and are, ill-prepared.

Society appears to often deem one and all ready for love as much as it deems all parents as loving, rarely contemplating there are those with limited capacity for love. Not once in my entire childhood did I ever question my parents capacity for love; instead I internalized their lack of capacity as my lack of lovability. This is a core legacy of growing up in an alcoholic and violent environment.

There are those who do the opposite, however. This is only my story, which is the only one I can tell, so I internalized a profound disbelief in my own lovability. This unfortunate childhood experience tends to leave a dysfunctional legacy of love, leaving the adult child without adequate skills, experience, knowledge, or judgment for loving situations. Without proper treatment, this shortcoming is passed onto the next generation with or without the presence of alcohol. Herein lies an even more insidious version of dysfunction when dysfunction is passed to the next generation without the presence of alcohol, making detection and treatment not easy.

One day hopefully there will be literature on the distinct nuances of intergenerational dysfunction for adult children of alcoholics, violence, and dysfunction. However until then we are left with a dangerous reality.

Chapter Six

Avoidance of the Truth Is Rarely Love

In the alcoholic home in which I grew up there were unwritten commandments. Many of those commandments had to do with the way we interpreted what we experienced in daily life. It had to do with how we perceived reality. There were things that we perceived as being more important than an accurate awareness of what was going on. Those things were:

- The way we thought things should be
- The way we wanted things to be
- The way we needed things to be

In my family we had a very low threshold for things being as they were, especially when contrary to the commandments above. At some times our tolerance level for disparity was and can only be described as zero tolerance.

If there was to be any deviation from these cardinal interpretations, those variations were *never* to come from children. It was not so much that children were suppose to be seen and not heard as it was that when children were heard it was expected to be something that was tolerable, comfortable, non-challenging, and supportive of the status quo. Children were expected to be the support system of the fantasy, never to challenge it. Deviation from this rule could be, and often was, met with verbal or physical abuse so the consequences of any deviation from the commandments/model made the endeavor not worth the punishment.

The first cardinal rule, "the way we thought things should be," was usually specifically idealized by my mother, i.e., we were always to be the ideal family on the outside regardless of what was actually going on inside the family or within the confines of that house.

There was many a Sunday that we stood in church all in the same pew in our Sunday-best clothing that hid bruises and wounds acquired the night before from a night of alcoholism and violence. Often during these Sunday mornings the hardest thing for me to do was to hold my eyes open as a result of being up all night with police officers and emergency personnel. Yet as we left the church we would all parade out in unison with smiles on our faces and depression, despair, anger, pain and resentment in our hearts.

Paradoxical as it may seem, the one place where it might appear to be the most useful to unload this heap of emotions was the most taboo of all places, and the most important place for us all to appear to be in good stead. Somehow we all knew that church was the place that demanded our best acting and we performed well with years of rehearsals. The way we thought things should be was always paramount over the way things actually were.

The "way we wanted things to be" was a dream/fantasy that I do believe each and every member of my family participated in. The fantasy contained our fondest hopes, dreams, and aspirations for the family. It was only that we rarely were able to get anywhere near the reality of those dreams. Our dreams/fantasies mostly remained just that, fantasies, with no basis in reality or behavior. We dreamed of being a loving family, we wanted to be a loving family, we hoped to be a loving family, however mostly we were verbally abusive, neglectful, ignorant of each other's needs, ignorant that needs even existed, typically violent and drunken, especially on the weekends.

We never once had a family discussion concerning the way we actually were, other than my mother's constant rants concerning my father's drinking, which in reality did not bother me much. I was much more concerned with the constant ass whippings and verbal abuse I received from my mother than anything else that ever went on in that house.

The way we needed things to be was probably the most complex and confusing of all our fantasies. It was full of paradoxes that ultimately made no sense. On the one hand, I suspect we all wanted peace, at least I know we children did. However there were obvious times when the peace was intentionally disturbed by my mother, which I have not understood until this day. It was almost as if on some level there was an actual need for chaos, or maybe a better way to explain it is that we had a real need for something to complain about at all times, and this need existed within each family member at one time or another. As children we were learning to emulate our parents.

There was no shortage of judgment, criticism, second-guessing, and punishment in that environment. There was always a lack of acceptance, forgiveness, tolerance, understanding, curiosity, or active and effective communication between each and every one of us.

Considering my family was ruled by:

- The way we thought things should be
- The way we wanted things to be
- The way we needed things to be

The potential for us to perceive, evaluate, discuss, and work through any issue was less than nil. As a result, our problems and issues grew in intensity throughout the years and the emotional distance between us amplified exponentially. That expanse of emotional distance for the most part has never ceased. I am unsure if it can ever be repaired once the distance becomes so great; maybe there is only so much that can be made up for in a lifetime. I am unsure, however; for me it has always felt as if something maybe unidentifiable was missing.

One of the most surprising shocks of my life, however, was on the day my father told me that he never loved me. In that moment all the emotional distance of a lifetime seemed to fade away. In that moment I did not feel distant from him. I have always thought it paradoxical that he was telling me that he never loved me and I actually felt close to him closer than I ever had before. *It was a unique feeling, but it was what I had been searching for all my life. Whatever it was that I had always sought and needed from my daddy was there when he told me he never loved me.*

I guess it was the first time between us that we did not seek to avoid reality. The paradox is being told that I had never been loved actually felt loving; more importantly it felt honest, sane, and authentic. It was a peaceful moment in a relationship of turmoil!

If I have learned anything from growing up in a home riddled with alcoholism, violence, and dysfunction, it is the importance of being able to identify and ask the right question. Without the right question, no matter what answer we arrive at will not be the answer that will be most effective in providing a solution for the most pertinent issues tearing the family apart. A question not based in truth cannot yield positive results within the truth. As a result, the emotional distance within the family tends to increase the harder we work on issues. This always was a level of insanity that as a child I seemed to recognize. However, I could never quite wrap my mind all the way around it. All I knew was that with time things were getting worse in spite of my best efforts and, apparently, in spite of the best efforts of those around me.

I have an analogy for my family that is perfect. We all lived in a house where the roof was on fire. In addition, there was a step missing from the front porch, a hole in a screen door, a leaky kitchen faucet, and a plugged drain in the bath-room. We all were aware of all these items and from time to time we would attempt to repair the missing front step or the leaky faucet or some other repair. However at all cost we never, ever would attempt to put out the fire on the roof.

We ignored the fire on the roof at all cost even as the smoke filled our lungs and made it more difficult to breath. The more difficult it became to breath the more we denied that the roof was on fire and would brag about what a good job we were doing repairing the missing step or fixing the leaky faucet.

This was my family. From outside the family we may have

sounded crazy, however from within it was just the way we operated and we knew no other way to behave, so we continued to do what we thought was best as we choked from the smoke and became debilitated.

As a way of living, this developed an extremely high threshold for pain in the family and especially in the children, because it was our foundation and education of how to exist. We were raised not to recognize pain and to quite literally interpret pain as normal, because for us intense familial pain had always been normal. We knew nothing else.

I suspect we often interpreted this pain as love because it denoted an intensity or passion of effort. In an environment that lacked free flowing emotions almost any emotion was often welcomed. It was good to simply know that one was not dead.

The concept of talking through a tough reality and facing the consequences was beyond our ability to accept. In order for that to occur, someone in the family would have had to face the damages occurring right in our midst as a result of alcoholism, and although it was right in front of us, our ability to grasp it as an issue, hold onto to it, and talk our way through it was beyond our skill level. Since this was the only modeled behavior for the children, it was what we learned and rarely questioned. We could rarely deal with truth as it presented itself. We could not deal with life on life's terms.

As difficult as it may be, I have now grown to know that love can rarely be demonstrated without a serious confrontation, ownership, exploration, and evaluation of the perceived reality before us. In an alcoholic family there is no way for this to occur because we do not have the tools or the skill set to pull off such an achievement. Unfortunately anything else other than this talk and walk through reality or truth is typically an illusion or delusion, as much as we may wish it otherwise.

Rarely is true loved not based in reality. I think love is simply truth at all cost for most state of affairs.

Chapter Seven

Sacrifice And Love

There are times that walking through the truth is just too painful and challenging for an alcoholic and violent family, especially for the children. In many circumstances it is more than a child can bear.

The denial system that is unrelenting in an alcoholic family trains children in the convoluted process of accepting a harmful status quo. Children who grow up in this kind of a system rarely develop the skills to perceive, process, or do anything about harmful dangerous or shitty realities. Since the function of the family system is to allow dysfunction, children are unconsciously trained to sustain dysfunction in their lives without even knowing it. Without treatment this tendency can sustain itself throughout a lifetime.

Since the adult child has been taught since birth to ignore or deny harmful reality as it presents itself, the adult child is essentially at a loss or disadvantage since he lacks a critical life skill, or especially at crucial moments when prompt action is a necessity. The adult child is, in effect, emotionally disabled for all intents and purposes.

The situation is further complicated by the fact that the adult child of an alcoholic typically sees him or herself as actually the opposite, as one who can see, analyze, and endure more than most. I once heard a remark that exemplifies what this does to the personality of the adult child of an alcoholic: "Adult children of alcoholics rush in where angels fear to tread." What is meant by this is that we do not see inherent challenges, let alone dangers and risks in many situations because we were raised with insurmountable challenges and dangers, so for us it is normal or not outside our realm of what we would consider normal. The consequence is that often our decision-making capacity is not as competent as it could be or even needs to be given many situations.

Since our capacity for evaluating and analyzing reality is off-center, it puts us at a considerable disadvantage when it comes to recognizing, and evaluating love, especially in its functional form, since we have so little experience with love in its functional form.

We operate without the benefit of an active, proven, functioning model, which is itself a considerable shortcoming. We are left with attempting to achieve that which we have never seen, felt, or experienced.

As a result, we often depend on the tools we perfected in childhood for seeing the reality we need to see, seeing the reality we want to see, seeing the reality we think we should see, rather than seeing reality simply as it is. It is a form of repetition compulsion that is attractive to the degree of being addictive. It is not that there are not other choices; we are unaware of those choices.

Lacking the ability to see things as they are gives adult children of alcoholics a shortcoming that perpetuates dysfunction throughout a lifetime.

In order to make my point I need to arrive at a reasonable definition of love. No definition would ever be near adequate, so I will work with what I have for purposes of this work.

Now we have to raise a question. Is childhood a frivolous tenure that has to be endured, or can it actually serve an emotional, mental, physical, and spiritual purpose preparing us to make contributions throughout life? If the latter is true, then this training must serve the purpose of teaching children how to walk through various realities or truths, since none of us knows what the future may hold. We can reasonably assume that in a human life some of those realities will be wonderful and enchanting and some will be dreadful and horrible and everything that could ever possibly be in between.

If we do not adequately train children to walk through all manner of realities or truth then we have not prepared them for the task of handling the vicissitudes of a responsible life. Therefore one of the responsibilities of parental love has to be: "Preparing children to functionally walk and talk through life's realities as they may present themselves." This teaches children to navigate life on life's terms.

It is not loving to rear children not to deal with reality or truth. Yet, the training received in alcoholic, violent, and dysfunctional homes trains children to do just that: ignore, deny, minimize, intellectualize, rationalize, avoid realities that are uncomfortable. This cannot be love!

In the home in which I was raised, we had no idea that love often is built on sacrifice. We were more concerned with the fact that we often needed or wanted it to feel good as opposed to being useful.

The sacrifices that were needed the most were not identifiable to my parents as issues. As a child I knew two things: I knew my father needed to stop drinking and I knew my mother needed to stop being violent. These I would have perceived as tremendous improvements in my family, but neither of my parents felt the same way. My mother perceived my father's drinking as a problem, but he did not see it that way. My father perceived my mother's violence as an issue because he was the chief victim of it but she did not see it that way. With all the blood that was shed in that home, she always thought her violence was necessary. She beat my father, my sister, and me, and somehow in her mind she thought she was doing a good thing. Or maybe that is just something I still needed to believe but it does not change the bottom line that her violence was as damaging as his drinking if not more so.

For him to stop drinking or for her to stop being violent would have required sacrifice, and these would have been the most loving things they could have done for the family. However the idea of making that degree of sacrifice on behalf of the family was a concept far beyond our family's reach.

My mother would talk about loving her family to the women of the church and talk about the sacrifice of not being able to buy a dress. However she was unwilling to forsake her first love which was her violent nature. Her sense of sacrifice involved what she could brag about sacrificing on behalf of her children to her friends. It was rarely about quiet untold sacrifices.

My father never put up the pretense that he was going to sacrifice on behalf of his family, and on more than one occasion he would readily admit that he would stop drinking as soon as they stopped making alcohol. Sacrifice as a foundation of love was not within our realm of consideration.

Chapter Eight

Shitty Realities and Grandiose Fantasies

Grandiose is a peculiar way to describe the illusions of growing up in a home of alcoholism, violence, and dysfunction, however it is the best word I can come up with to describe the promises and my inner emotional reactions as I listened to each parental promise. We were always going to be happy somewhere, somehow, in the future. Those promises were never about the here and now or about what we were going to do with the present moment.

There was a charming grandiosity with each promise at the time the promise was being made, and the child I was not only believed in every promise but wanted to believe, needed to believe, and thought I should believe; even after promise, after promise, after promise was broken, and broken, and broken. The more broken promises I heard, the harder I believed, the harder I wanted to believe and the more I needed to believe. The child I once was wanted to believe my parents loved me enough to make their promises come true.

I wanted to believe they would make the promises come true more than I wanted to believe the realities of the patterns of behavior in front of me. It was only in therapy that I learned *patterns of behavior do not lie.*

There is no telling how many promises were made during my childhood. Some were for fun things, trips to the ballgame, the circus, or just trips to the corner Nickel and Dime Store. Unfortunately, I could not depend on my

parents for what in my mind were essential things, like remembering my birthday or that I was in a school play, or a school concert.
Worse yet were the promises that were not made that could have been made. I promise not to knock you out again, I promise not to bloody your nose again, I promise not to attack you with a knife again. However, during such rare moments there were always declarations of love, especially from my mother; my wiping blood from my body was always met with the most tender reminder that it was for my own good. Whenever there was bloodshed it was always for my own good and it was always a result of her fondness and compassion for my welfare. This never once lessened the pain of being beaten in childhood, however it did instill a degree of guilt in being beaten, because it was always made readily apparent that my being beaten was my own fault. As a child I experienced guilt in addition to physical pain in those moments and it was more than I could handle. I could never once figure out why I continually caused my own pain and it drove me insane in the attempt to figure it out. Yet, I knew it was my own fault because my mother told me it was my fault.

The grandiose charm of the love affair between parent and child was often intense, especially with my mother; it overwhelmed me, consumed me, and allured me in every way. I wanted to be in love with my parents, I needed to be in love with my parents, and more than anything thought that I should be in love with my parents. Over the years the pain I endured at their hands, especially my mother, started to little by little squeeze the love out of my heart. It was replaced with anger, resentment, fear, anxiety, rage, and delusions of every kind. It was not so much that I started to not love my parents as it was that I ran out things to give. I was running out of the energy to tirelessly nurture and support them. Their needs were endless and unceasing and I was growing tired. The older I grew the more I came to realize that I was not an endless supply line of what it was they needed. I saw my father as rather helpless and my mother as rather mean, vindictive, and vengeful and I was running out of resources to handle either.

I will forever be at a loss to describe the pain of having the love of childhood squeezed out of my heart in innumerable, intolerable, excruciating moments. It is beyond description; each moment running into the next so they eventually became impossible to tell apart. It was a way of life!

My fantasies that my parents loved me appeared to be realistic and I did not perceive them as delusions. My beliefs in love were based on what had been taught to me; the neglect, abuse, broken promises, and lack of emotional availability were described to me as love and the behaviors were the only ones I had ever experienced, so when I was told it was love I accepted it was love, without question. I had no reason to believe my parents would lie. As a result my definition of love somehow, somewhere, someway always had an element of pain.

In later years when consistent pain was a part of relationships based upon my childhood experiences, I considered it normal, because it was what I had known. While I suspect most people would consider what I experienced in childhood as delusions of love, it had been defined to be truth and it was the only truth I had ever known, so it became my reality. I had challenges accepting a loving relationship that did not include pain based on what I had known.

If I was lucky enough to sustain a relationship that bordered on any type of an authentic love without some form of pain, my questions of its reality, its substance, its archetype, or its endurance were ceaseless. There were times the interminable lack of acceptance contributed to the demise of what was closest to functional love and help to turn the relationship more into what I had historically known.
This type of a long-term childhood fantasy created an emotional tendency not only to live in illusion but to readily create and accept fantasy as reality.

I suspect when one's childhood is fulfilled with the acceptance of fantasies, especially coming from one's parents, and the denial of reality, then the tolerance of truth evolves to be complex. For me in many situations it was.

A mirage is easier recognized as a mirage if one has had an opportunity to compare it to reality, and the denial system of growing up in alcoholism provided few opportunities for learning the skill of talking and walking through any reality, let alone a challenging reality.

The preferred way of living as a child with dysfunctional parenting is in the grandiose fantasies served daily by one's parents. It is a pseudo comfort, less stressful and more than anything it is all I knew. I had no basis of assessment compared to anything else.

In order to accept anything else as a truth would have forced the child I once was to talk and confront an excruciatingly painful reality before I was ready, and I had neither the skill nor the wherewithal to do such a thing. More importantly, I did not have the will, because what child knowingly has the ability to accept the reality of a lack of parental love. It would have been more to bear than the small shoulders I once possessed could have borne.

My childhood with an alcoholic daddy and a mentally ill, violent mama was certainly shitty. The child I once was needed and wanted to be loved, yet almost all of the messages I received from my parents could only be interpreted as I was unworthy of love.

I was constantly in a state of conflicted emotions. The older I became the more conflicted the emotions became. My incessant efforts to win their approval was an obsession that was all-consuming.

I was completely unable to handle the shitty truth in which I found myself on one level, however on another level I was surrounded by the consequences and dwelt with those consequences time and again.

My mother's fondest wish certainly was that my daddy stop drinking, or at least slow up some. I was not as bothered by my father's drinking as I was by my mother's violence. It was not that I could not see the damage done by the drinking, it was more that I was tired of getting beat up and witnessing others in the family getting beat up, so in my mind that was the tip of the spear. *For me the beatings caused more pain than the drinking ever did.*

Our family was being torn apart on two fronts: one of

drinking and the other constant violence. If in fact my father was addicted to alcohol, them my mother was certainly addicted to violence, and each member of my family bears scars as witness.

Until this day I am still uncertain how a child maneuvers through such a shitty reality that I was raised in. I had no good ideas at the time, and I still have none. Life was simply an uncontrollable attempt to survive.

The energy and effort necessary to maintain safety and sanity in that environment robbed me of intellect, energy, hopes, goals, and aspirations, because my mind was worried with tactics or strategies for survival for the next emergency that always came. Intense anxiety was my never-ending loyal companion and best friend.

I was afraid to let my mind drift too far away from the struggle of growing up in that home because I might not be prepared for the next drunken fight, hospital run, call to the police, or knifing by my mother, so there was a part of me always mired in the swampland of dysfunction which was my home. The constant worry became a way of living which appeared necessary for all practical intents and purposes. There was never a time to let one's guard down. There was rarely a time to relax!

When I left that home and entered other environments, the worrying left that home with me. It was my way of being in the world. I knew nothing else. When that level of intense worry is not necessary based upon current realities, it is typically known as neurosis, and I had no way of ridding myself of a necessary survival neurosis I had practiced and perfected for years.

While I still lived in that home I may have had the resources to confront and walk though the shitty reality or truths, however my greatest obstacle was always going to be my parents who were always my strongest leaders into fantasies of what our family was, what we wanted it be, what we needed it to be, or what we thought it should be.

The child I once was could not stand up to my parents emotionally, mentally, spiritually, and, most of all, physically, since confrontation with truth as it was presented by my parents was typically a guarantee for a physical reprisal.

I learned how to live within a shitty reality, how to believe the fantasy was real, how to defend the fantasy against outside reality, and how to nurture and support the fantasy at all cost.

This was the price of the approval of my parents, who typically made it readily known that any conflict with their perception of truth would meet with dire consequences. As a result, our family never mastered the skill of discussion of varying interpretations of reality that could be merged into functional family growth.

We harbored anger, rage, fear, and resentment at any interpretation of anything that did not meet with certain interpretations. My mother's favorite name for me whenever I brought up any idea that did not agree with her own was always "dumb stupid jackass." As a result I abandoned any imaginative or creative ways to look at the world and developed a hypersensitivity to her interpretations to ensure I would always be on the right side of any conflict. This did increase my measure of safety, however, at the cost of having any original ideas, thoughts, or feelings of my own. I started to kill the real or creative and imaginative self for the sake of safety.

I swallowed not only my pride but my dignity, my self-esteem, and my own individual sense of self. I killed the emotional, mental, and spiritual to protect the physical. *I killed my inner emotional world for the sake of safety.*

Chapter Nine

Talking and Walking Through a Shitty Reality

As I started healing, I slowly but surely started to talk and walk through uncomfortable realities I had avoided for years, however as a concept the bell had not yet rung for me. The idea of talking and walking through a shitty reality as an act of love would be a concept I would not learn until therapy became more ingrained in my life.

I put together the concept that if reality is not effectively dealt with, I could not personally develop. However what really struck me on an emotional, mental, and spiritual level was one day in therapy when my therapist looked at me and said, "Sometimes reality is shitty, but it's all we got."

Maybe I was just ready to accept or hear it that day but the harshness of that truth hit me; *reality is all we got.* There have been few times in my life that a moment changed it forever. My experience has been spiritual, mental, and emotional awakening is a slow, gradual process, however in that moment my life changed and has never been the same.

Having a childhood of avoiding shitty realities at all cost does nothing to effectively train an individual to talk and walk through shitty realities or truths, yet, there are many shitty realities that can only be talked and walked through in order to get to the other side, or to get better. The avoidance of reality has never had the same strength ever since the moment my therapist made that comment. It has been a huge improvement in the way I choose to live my life. In that moment I realized I have choices far beyond anything I had ever known.

Had this concept been presented earlier in my life I doubt if I could have or would have seen the value, which brings me to an important point. As a result of therapy I have learned that *one has to be ready and willing to grow.* To make that big leap across the divide and to the next way of walking and talking. It's like jumping off the high diving board and unsure if there is any water in the pool. Any type of change requires courage, and for those of us who grew up in homes of emotional and mental rigidity we lack models of the courage to change.

Because of the way I had been raised, the concept of being ready for growth or change was a foreign concept to me. I had never been asked if I was ready to take on new responsibility throughout my childhood.

Typically, new responsibility came as a demand from my mother or because my father was drunk and something had to be done and done immediately. It was not a matter of whether I could rise to the occasion, I had to rise to the occasion regardless of my fears, concerns, lack of preparation, or inability to have any idea as to what I was doing. This was the way I was taught during my childhood for anything from erecting a play set, to gardening, to painting. It was what I had modeled for me and it was what I often thought to be appropriate.

There was rarely any consideration as to whether the skills required were within my physical, emotional, or mental capacity. That is one of the characteristics of being raised in alcoholism and violence; there is rarely any consideration of the emotional, mental or physical. For all practical purposes, it is as if those considerations do not exist for children in that environment. In effect, children exist for the purposes of the perpetuation of the dysfunction. Children are molded, groomed, trained, and educated to support, nurture, and enhance dysfunction.

There is a reason why school is a consecutive process. There is the building of a foundation and the acquisition of skills built upon a logical consecutive foundation. This type of consideration and skill set does not exist in the home riddled with alcoholism and violence because the compulsion or obsession is what attention is paid to, certainly not the developmental needs of the children. This presents consequences to the lives of the children. Unless treated, those consequences can be life-long and worsen long after the individual has left that environment.

The idea of being ready to take on additional responsibility is a nurturing concept in itself, and nurturing is in short supply in an alcoholic and violent environment. As a result, children are often rushed into adult responsibilities before being ready, which often leads to its own unique aversion to responsibility. In other words, another unique neurosis from excessive drinking and violence.

One of the most important considerations or realizations I have come to when it comes to my alcoholic family is that as much as my parents probably wanted to love their children, they quite literally could not.

Many of the things represented by them they thought were love. I am unsure as to what degree of choice either of my parents had at the time and that is the saddest state of affairs for my family or any family.

As much as we denied, minimized, rationalized, intellectualized, or avoided the truth of the reality concerning our family, I do believe it was all we knew how to do. Since denial was a part of our ingrained system, we were not about to take in or let in any new information that may have been helpful. Quite to the contrary, for the most part we perceived new information as a threat.

So far as the functioning of the family was concerned, new information actually would have been a threat and one which we did not know how to admit into our psyche, let alone put to good use in allowing our family to be more loving.

So in our heart of hearts we perceived denial, avoidance, minimization, intellectualization, or rationalization of truth as the most loving behavior we could come up with, which at the time it obviously was.

Chapter Ten

The Most Authentic Gift of Love: The Gift of Self

Growing up in alcoholism, violence, and dysfunction left me with countless reservations concerning the nature of love: degree of love, quality of love, does love always hurt, does love always have to feel good, did love exist in my home.

Those could be questions all people have concerning childhood. I have no way of knowing; all I know is I had bewildering uncertainties and had no realistic way of discovering useful answers. As a result I often made reticent resolutions without input in stressful situations, as I learned to do in childhood.

After I became an adult I tended to keep a lot of significant considerations concerning a practical and realistic way to live at bay, arm's length, so to speak. It was a subject that I knew existed but I just didn't want to deal with the issue. I was too lazy and too scared to deal with the subject. My fear stemmed from the fact that if I discovered information that was new, what would I do? I was always afraid. My childhood was not one of allowing in new information, since as a family we had a rigid system of existence. We were always in protection of the status quo, always in protection of the alcoholism, the violence, and the dysfunction.

There is nothing more fearful for most adult children of alcoholics than to enter into the unknown, especially alone. We have had a life-time of entering into the unknown alone for most of life's most significant and meaningful experiences. The unknown often consisted of things like the strange nature or characteristics of life, e.g., peace, incest, molestation, violence, love, resentment, hatred, betrayal, trust, loyalty and a never-ending list of questionable feelings as a result of living an entire childhood in the midst of the uncertainty. Lack of stability and consistency is the nature of the alcoholic, violent, or dysfunctional childhood. Disturbingly, the lack of stability and consistency come mostly from those we depended on the most to provide stability and consistency.

Maybe raising children in alcoholism, violence, and dysfunction is basically a betrayal of the children and the trust they inherently have in parents. There is an inheritance from growing up in an alcoholic home of neurosis, anxiety, worry, panic, obsession and compulsion; and *most of our inheritance is on an unconscious level.*

The questions of my parents that I most wanted answers to I did not have the courage to ask until after I had been in therapy for about a year. At that point the questions changed from something I had put off for years to something that had a pressing urgency.

My questions concerning the nature of love were directed at my parents, who I perceived as my primary life guides.

I had always experienced their love as consuming without benefit of replenishment, and by the time I was a teenager I was running low on anything to continue to give without hurting myself. It was as if my parents constantly needed me and the rest of their children as a hostage audience for whatever their neurosis of the day would be; yet they provided no audience for the concerns of their children. I came to a point where it was not that I did not care for my parents, I just had no more to give.

I do not know if I ever really met my mother. If she had any vulnerabilities I did not know of any. It was almost as if everything I ever saw of her was only what she wanted me to see and what she allowed me to see did nothing to let me see vulnerabilities. Without vulnerabilities I saw no need to love, as she was wrapped securely within her own power.

At the same time I adored her. She was tough, she lacked weaknesses of any kind, she had immediate answers to everything. What I adored the most I also hated. The best I can say about our mother-son relationship is that it was frequently conflicted. I adored her and I hated her!

My parents had different or varying ways in which they felt about love.

In my family there existed several characteristics of what we defined as love.

<u>Characteristics of Love Within Alcoholism, Violence and Dysfunction</u>:

1. My parents passed to me what had been passed to them.
2. My parents could not love me effectively because they could not love themselves adequately.
3. My parents were severely wounded.
4. My parents had a very limited capacity to love, especially themselves.
5. Being aware of parental shortcomings is a prerequisite

of truth and functionality.
6. The gift is within me.

When I was a young child I perceived my parents as deities. For me they had all answers. While my father was indifferent to this admirable affection, my mother nurtured and demanded this adoration, and as I became older and started to sometimes question the nature of her needs, there were consequences to be paid in terms of resentments, anger, and retribution of many kinds for any lack of respect or inquiry into her always unquestionably right and honorable opinion. There could be no other respected opinion in the home other than her own.

1. <u>My parents passed on to me what had been passed on to them</u>

On the day I questioned my father about the nature of his love for me, he told me a story from his childhood. The spirit of the story was spontaneous, sincere, warm, and for the first time in our relationship I came to realize that he was as confused as to the nature of love as I was.

He had questions concerning the nature of the parenting he received during his childhood, and I realized that since he had never resolved these matters concerning his own childhood that we would never be able to answer the questions concerning the way I was raised, because he had not come within reach of the concern for himself. Since he had not provided resolution for himself, he could not for anyone else, especially his children.

He, like me, had kept the issue at arm's length. It was a

touching moment of vulnerability to recognize in him; it made me feel close to him in a way I had rarely felt.

I came to realize in that moment that much of the way he treated me was the way he had been treated, and that although he questioned the way he had been treated, he never took the time to change or even challenge what he perceived as injurious to his own childhood. He could do no better with raising me because he had never challenged his own upbringing to make the necessary adjustments for improvement, even though he had many questions concerning the functionality of his own parenting.

I believe what he and I were discussing on that summer afternoon can only be called intergenerational transfer of dysfunction, and the subject was larger than our combined minds were able to grasp.

There was much of my parents I did not understand as a child. My father's habit of getting falling down drunk never made sense to me. My mother's habit of whipping on him when he did never made sense to me, especially since he was the biggest and strongest person in the household. While it was extremely rare for him to exert any of that physical strength, hitting on him unprovoked always appeared to be unwise behavior.

2. <u>My parents could not love me effectively because they could not love themselves adequately.</u>

My parents did a fairly poor job of loving themselves for the majority of their lives. I have come to believe they could not have loved their children any better than they had loved themselves.

There is a phrase from the Bible: I have heard often; "love thy neighbor as thyself." However when it comes to my parents that would not have been a wise phrase to use since neither of them appeared to love themselves well. Each demonstrated self- defeating behaviors on a consistent long-term basis.

I do not believe any reasonably healthy human being would have demonstrated the behaviors that were paramount to my parents lives unless they were severely wounded. When considering my parents capacity for love it is important to consider they each had little capacity for loving themselves.

I was middle-aged before I realized that all the times when my father was falling down drunk and I would cook his dinner, clean up after him, or tuck him into bed, no one was taking care of me at the time. We had the roles reversed.

The same goes for all the times when I would have intense discussions with my mother into the wee hours of the morning trying to arrive at reasonable solutions for her many problems, not one of those discussions ever rallied around any issue that I was having at the time. Most of my childhood was without parental input for my issues. It was as if I and my siblings were their parents. I do not say this to complain, because it was just the way that it was, and I did it because I wanted to do it. But I did it also because I cared and wanted to be useful.

I also wonder how is it that any reasonable parent would never consider that their child may have any issue that needs discussion. I was raised and educated to be at their emotional, mental, and physical service as a responsibility of existence. Anything other than that would have subjected me to their disapproval, and at the time I lived for my parents' approval, acceptance, and love, which for the most part always felt as if it were unreachable and completely conditional.

I do not think they were able to love themselves for several reasons. First, people who love themselves do not get drunk daily, and second, people who love themselves do not beat their husband and children on a regular basis. It was almost as if my mother hated most what she created.

My parents could not love their children because they could not love themselves, and their children were a part of them as they perceived it.

3. <u>My parents were severely wounded.</u>

It has always been my sense that my father's source of wounding came from having grown up in an alcoholic, violent, and dysfunctional household.

My mother rarely talked about herself on any kind of emotionally intimate level, so I have always felt that on an emotional, mental, and spiritual level I never really knew the woman. I am truly at a loss to even guess the source of her wounding. I did meet her father once, however my sense of that meeting was that there was this strange man who was trying to be nice to me, who I did not know and did not feel comfortable around. I was about six years old at the time.

My mother who always proclaimed her feeling of never-ending love for her children would be very disappointed in most of what I have written here. She constantly proclaimed her love for her children, however rarely in a matter-of-fact kind of way. It was always a proclamation for all those around her at the time to pay attention to and pay homage to such a noble woman. It felt as if her proclamation of love needed an audience and needed more than the children she reported to love.

It always felt as if the proclamation was of some form of self-interest to her in some way that I could never define or wrap my childhood mind around.

My reality for my childhood is I rarely if ever felt loved and for my childhood self, love unfelt is love unrealized. Love unfelt for me was useless, because it did not exist in my heart.

I know my mother did not grow up in a regular family and seemed to harbor some type resentment against both of her parents, but other than that I know nothing.

My parents were constantly hurting themselves, each other, or their children, which appears to be the result of people who are themselves in pain.

4. <u>My parents had a very limited capacity to love, especially themselves</u>

What my parents declared as love I have come to oppose and no longer see such behavior as loving.

Wrapped up in such intense proclamations of love and on-going contrary feelings of pain was a high degree of on-going insanity that I could never really rid myself of.

My father's talk with me saying he never loved me has been of great assistance. It freed me to search for a more generous, less painful, more nurturing, more supportive definition. This freedom contributed greatly to a feeling of increased sanity in my life.

My childhood always felt as if it had a high degree of insanity because none of it rarely made sense. The people who were trying to parent me were helpless in and of themselves, so whatever it was they were trying to teach always felt as if it was a lesson they had not yet learned themselves.

I think self-discipline has to be an element of self-love, and neither of my parents exemplified a sense of discipline in their lives and this limited their capacity to love themselves and their children.

The idea of love having anything to do with sacrifice as a foundation of love was a concept lost in my family. The love I was taught was self-centered, undisciplined, and most of the time self-serving. My parents appeared to be their own worst enemies and it felt as if much of the time they also felt as if their children were their enemies because their children got in the way of their lives, because their children had needs, and meeting those needs required sacrifice.

Although my parents were adults, they could not meet their own needs so they could not meet the needs of their children. It would be an unreasonable and unrealistic expectation to place upon them. Yet it was a responsibility that comes with children at the moment of birth.

5. <u>Being aware of parental shortcomings is a prerequisite of truth and functionality.</u>

The idea of parental shortcomings is sensitive, to say the least. Many may consider it disrespectful to consider parental shortcomings; however, I have come to believe it is a necessity in evaluating the how and why of moving a family forward into functionality.

As a child I was certainly punished for ever bringing forth anything that could even remotely be considered a parental short-coming. However, what that taught me to do was to be in denial of grave aspects of the truth that were harmful. It would have been much more advantageous to be taught how to own, confront, talk and walk through short-comings, especially from a parent, since it may have been the most effective way of teaching children how to talk and walk through uncomfortable realities.

Most important in the consideration of parental short-comings is the fact that there will always exist within ourselves the possibility that in evaluating parental short-comings we will most likely find a considerable amount of our own. How could that not be? It is our parents or primary caregivers who had the primary involvement is shaping us. We are and will always be tied to those we came from, however that does not mean that we cannot re-sculpt what has been sculpted.

It is our primary spiritual, emotional, and mental responsibility to sculpt our existence into whatever we would like it to be. Otherwise we allow ourselves to become victims of things which have long since passed away.

The process of healing is most certainly a process of the acceptance of responsibility for what we are responsible for and oftentimes for what we inherited. However the bottom line is still the same, it is our responsibility. Since we came from a family system of denial, we will always have a more difficult time identify truth, especially when it is an uncomfortable truth; however it does not mean we are helpless. It simply means there is work to be done.

At the beginning I experienced the work as painful, because I had to re-live so many of the experiences I had emotionally, spiritually, and mentally denied as a child. Secondly, it was painful in accepting my own short-comings, which I had denied as an adult. However there was a dawn in the far-off future that I was unable to see in the beginning.

What I was unable to see was as I came closer to the truth and started to become more of the person I wanted and needed to be, healing could and would become fun.

My greatest source of pain has become my greatest source of inspiration. That does not mean that there are not things I am not still afraid of. However, it does mean I now realize there is a good possibility there will be joy on the other side and in those times where there is not joy on the other side there is always peace.

There is a huge difference between my experiences of joy and of peace. Joy has been a satisfaction with the way that things turned out from whatever turmoil I perceived was going on.

Peace has tended to be deeper, more significant, meaningful, and lasting. I have generally experienced peace from turmoil when the situation did not turn out as I originally wanted it to turn out or needed it to turn out or thought is should turn out. However somehow I came to be at peace with the way things did turn out. Often in these situations the turmoil may have ended in my worst imaginary case scenario, which was now real but what changed in the process was me.

There has been no other experience in my life that has taught me the essence of vulnerability and humility better than this. Vulnerability and humility often afford me the gift of not being attached to the outcome and to cherish being in the moment, whatever the moment. As I once heard a long time ago, "this too will change." What I did not realize at the time was that within the comment "this too will change" is the possibility that what will change is me, if I allow it.
My realizations of my parents' short-comings and my own had always been a direct guidance system into truth and therein lies reality. We all experience reality differently; however, as humans it is necessary for us all to share our experiences, otherwise we leave our versions

of the reality out of the equation of consideration. That is what happened perpetually during my childhood, so there was only one version of the reality of experiences in that home and that version of the reality was always incomplete. As egocentric beings, we all have a tendency to do this; it is just that when the outside poisons of alcoholism, violence, and dysfunction are entered into consideration, we lose our sense of balance, which is the essence of truth with us all.

6. The gift is within me.

The most profound gift I can give myself is to not break from the vicissitudes of growing up in alcoholism, violence, and dysfunction and to integrate that experience into my life while learning to use it as a source of growth. It is my responsibility alone; however one of the things I had to learn is how to ask for help. It is my responsibility to grow beyond what I am in any given moment and to grow beyond whatever my parents ever were.

I wonder if people who grow up in more functional homes feel the same way; however from within my home it feels as if it is a spiritual mission to grow beyond that into which I was born.

There is much I do not know concerning the history of my family however I do know that the generation I was born into paid a horrendous price for the disease of alcoholism, violence, and dysfunction of the generation before. Furthermore I know the generation before me paid a horrible price for the alcoholism, violence, and dysfunction of the generation before them. It has to stop, of that I am certain, and I choose to say. It stops with me!

Some people are broken by the vicissitudes of growing up in alcoholism, violence, and dysfunction. They have given up on life and no longer have hopes, dreams, and aspirations.

I understand this way of living in an experiential way, as I have been there, where the pain of existence was such that I questioned if the efforts of survival were worth the returns, often longing for an end to the pain. Twice during the course of my life I attempted to end the pain, and there but for the grace of a benevolent creator, I would not be writing now. As a result, I have become a pragmatist about that particular subject and hold to the realization that for me if I had to live in that kind of pain again with *no hope of change*, ending it all would make perfect sense.

For the rest of us who are not broken to that point (since most of us are wounded) we can choose to move forward as best we can, moment by moment, seeking truth wherever we can. It takes a tremendous amount of courage to face the realities of our families, our parents, and ourselves, and it is an individual choice that each of us can and usually do make, since not making a choice is also making a choice.

There are many ways to move forward in healing, so I will not do any listing here other than make the recommendation of following the heart, since ultimately we all know when we are getting better and can often

differentiate when we are not. The peace of progress is undeniable! In situations where we cannot feel that peace we seek outside help.
I stand on the shoulders of my parents' souls. Though those shoulders were broken and wounded, I stand on them just the same. I stand on their shoulders as they stood on the shoulders of those who came before them.

I stand on those shoulders not in spite of the fact that those shoulders were broken and wounded, but because of the fact those shoulders were broken and wounded. It is the brokenness and the wounding that we are trying to heal.

In healing myself it becomes a self-fulfilling prophecy, because slowly but surely my life will always start to get better and I define better as spiritual, emotional, mental, and sometimes even physical healing, since we are systemically integrated organisms.

For me it has become a profound gift of healing, because from the distress of alcoholism, violence, and dysfunction I lost many things. What I lost and *what was most damaging more than anything else was the fact that I lost the ability to be me. I killed the real me and propagated the false me for the benefit of the dysfunctional family system into which I was born.*

It has been a long journey to recover those parts lost in the process of the disability of the disease, and I have had much help along the way, but it was, has been, and is doable.

I will not describe how the affects of alcoholism, violence

and dysfunction eats away at a child's soul because I feel my first book *Earning My Parents' Love* or 2nd Edition *Growing Up In Alcoholism, Violence & Dysfunction* describes this loss of the self in intimate detail. It will suffice to say that as a child loses parts of its soul to the dysfunction there becomes a spiritual imperative to do something about it, otherwise that loss is inadvertently and unconsciously passed to the next generation. More importantly, *losing parts of the soul we were meant to be has spiritual consequences that are larger than we can comprehend.*

We cannot not give what we do not possess, and if we do not have a calm, peaceful, and mature spirituality it becomes impossible to bequeath this to our children. It is like teaching our children to speak a language that we do not speak ourselves. Having said this, I do believe that there is no other entity in the universe that is more proud of the work I have done to heal myself than the man who I dedicate this book to, the man who had the courage to say he never loved me when I was a child, my father.

If there is such a thing as a soul or spirit then his can now say my sons' journey upon our spiritual healing happened not in spite of my life but because of my life. The short-comings of his life become a gift, because they became the seeds of growth, of spiritual awakening.

It was not his attempts to shield me from the adversities of realities that were the most potent seeds, it was his realization to share his most intimate reality that he never loved me that became the most potent seeds of awakening in my life.

In retrospect, I do not know if I would have developed

the ability to attempt to awaken without some effort at discovering truth or reality.

As I previously stated, my therapist once said to me, "Sometimes reality is shitty, but it's all we got." Since it is all we got then, in essence, it must always be the seed of growth or awakening, because anything else other than reality or truth has to be either a fantasy or a delusion, neither of which are real. More importantly, *our creator can only work miracles from a firmly grounded reality, not from delusion.*

My father who rarely loved me in this realm did start to love me in the moment he shared this truth, "I never loved you."

If there is such a thing as life after death, then I trust he is proud of his behavior in that moment of courage. I hope and trust he is proud of that one moment of truth that made all the other moments of pain and denial worthwhile, because in that moment we started to grow, to awaken, to evolve, and to heal. For the first time in our relationship we started to do these things together!

While I say he gave me the gift of truth I believe he also gave himself the gift of truth, the gift of courage and the gift of reality. I suspect it was not only a new beginning for me but also a new beginning for him. It allowed us to relate in a completely different way that was more free, relaxed, and authentic. I felt connected for the first time in a lifetime, a wonderful feeling for a son to share with a father. It was what I had been looking for all the long.

Growing up in a home of alcoholism, violence, and dysfunction is certainly difficult. It left me as a child empty, in despair, and desperate for love of any kind. I could hardly love myself because I had never been taught how to love myself and how could I have been?

Those who were raising me had never learned how to love themselves. From the child's point of view it leaves a perplexing impossibility, needing love and being untrained in creating, sustaining, or even identifying loving situations. I left that home is desperate need of love and ill prepared to handle the larger world-at-large. I did not know at the time was best said in a quote by Helen Keller, "What I am looking for is not out there, it is in me."

As a person raised to be dependent on not only others perceptions, but alcoholic, violent, and dysfunctional perceptions, this was a new concept to learn and bear in the journey of healing.

I believe my healing has spiritual consequences on my father's healing and his father's healing and his father before him. Our healing is unrelated and unrestricted to time and space since we are spiritual family. The healing of a world can start only within the healing of my own heart.

The End

EPILOGUE

It took me a long time to admit that I grew up without parental love. It was not that my parents chose not to love, I believe they never had a choice. What they believed was love was not however. It was in my childhood mind as it was in my parents' minds.

Today I have a more functional, soothing, comforting concept of love in which to blanket myself, and that makes all the difference in the world.

Notes

ABOUT THE AUTHOR

I was born in Newark, New Jersey. Most of my childhood experiences were in Newark, Harlem, New York, and the Bronx; I am the eldest of three children and I have an older sister I did not meet until age forty-six.

As a teenager I read Langston Hughes, Erich Maria Remarque, Maya Angelou, Ernest Hemingway, Stephen Crane, Countee Cullen, W.E.B. Du Bois, Nathaniel Hawthorne, Lorraine Hansberry, Charles Dickens, Mark Twain, Gwendolyn Brooks, Amiri Baraka, Arna Bontemps, and Jack London, to name a few favorites. I considered all of the above to be great storytellers. However my father had six brothers and the seven brothers enthralled the child I once was with the power of their storytelling. I learned at an early age that storytelling has the ability to transcend time and space. In my family there were stories of decades past where one could still smell the aroma of Georgia pine trees in the Bronx or the scent of apple pies cooked on stoves that burned wood long ago. I dreamed of being part of that community of storytellers and nothing makes me happier than a good story. I adore the magic of storytelling.

I have always enjoyed writing for as long as I can remember, dating back to a paper I wrote in college which was twelve typed pages entitled "Cross Elasticity's of Black Collegiate Demand" that I wrote for an economics class.

I've lived in almost a dozen states and today I live in

Escondido, California. I still possess a deep love for Tennessee, Kentucky, and Ohio. Or maybe those states remind me of enjoyable parts of the journey of my soul through life.

In my spare time I enjoy reading the newspaper by the ocean, playing piano, and I am still an avid reader. I have worked for several symphony orchestras during my life and enjoy classical music.

I also do guest speaking engagements at hospitals for medical students interested in the effects of growing up in alcoholism, violence, and dysfunction along with some churches and other organizations.

OTHER BOOKS BY MICHAEL WILLIAMS

GROWING UP IN ALCOHOLISM, VIOLENCE & DYSFUNCTION

LISTENING TO MY INNER CHILD

PAPERBACK AND KINDLE

THE WORKBOOK FOR GROWING UP IN ALCOHOLISM, VIOLENCE & DYSFUNCTION

WAKENING & LISTENING TO MY INNER CHILD

PAPERBACK

INSPIRATIONAL STORIES OF THE HOMELESS

DIGNITY, NOBILITY, DECENCY

PAPERBACK AND KINDLE

CURRENTLY AVAILABLE AT WWW.AMAZON.COM

www.ingramcontent.com/pod-product-compliance
Lightning Source LLC
Chambersburg PA
CBHW071638050426
42443CB00026B/721